THE HUMAN WORLD

the world in infographics

jon richards
and ed simkins

Owl kids

CONTENTS

WELCOME TO THE WORLD
OF INFOGRAPHICS

Using icons, graphics, and pictograms, infographics
visualize data and information in a whole new way!

**DISCOVER HOW MANY
PEOPLE THERE ARE FOR
EVERY CAR IN THE WORLD**

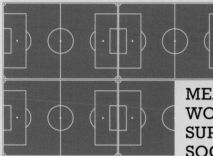

**MEASURE THE
WORLD'S LARGEST
SUPERMARKET IN
SOCCER FIELDS**

**SEE HOW MUCH
FOOD IS THROWN
AWAY EACH DAY**

COMPARE THE HEIGHT OF THE WORLD'S TALLEST BUILDINGS

MORE AND MORE PEOPLE

Improvements in diet and health care over the last hundred years have meant that many people are living for longer and fewer are dying young. This has led to an explosion in the world's population.

HOW MUCH LAND?

As the world's population has increased, the amount of land for each person has decreased.

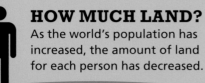

1900
0.03 MI.^{2}
(0.09 KM^2) EACH

1950
0.02 MI.^{2}
(0.06 KM^2) EACH

2010
0.008 MI.^{2}
(0.02 KM^2) EACH

2050
0.006 MI.^{2}
(0.016 KM^2) EACH

CITY VS. COUNTRY

Since 1800, more and more people have moved from the country to large cities.

3% — 97%
1800

47% — 53%
2000

60% — 40%
2030

THE WORLD'S POPULATION IS INCREASING BY

74,000,000

EVERY SINGLE YEAR.

DOUBLE TIME

The time it takes the world's population to grow by 1 billion has decreased. It took 32 years to grow from 2 billion to 3 billion, but it took only 13 years to grow from 6 billion to 7 billion.

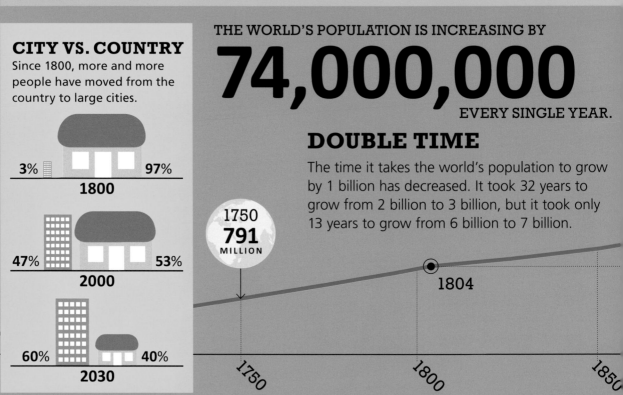

1750
791
MILLION

1804

1750

1800

1850

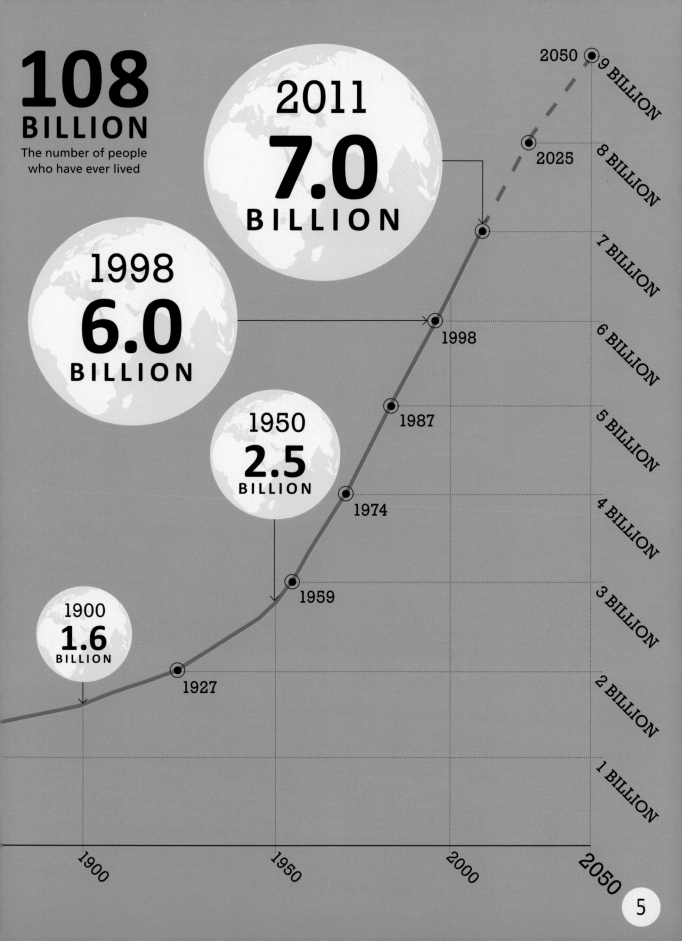

108 BILLION
The number of people who have ever lived

2011 7.0 BILLION

1998 6.0 BILLION

1950 2.5 BILLION

1900 1.6 BILLION

2050 — 9 BILLION
2025 — 8 BILLION
7 BILLION
1998 — 6 BILLION
1987 — 5 BILLION
1974 — 4 BILLION
1959 — 3 BILLION
1927 — 2 BILLION
1 BILLION

1900   1950   2000   2050

WHERE IN THE WORLD?

The distribution of the world's population is very uneven. While in some areas the average space each person has is the size of a small room, in others it can be the area of a town.

EUROPE
POPULATION
732,759,000
10.61%
OF WORLD
POPULATION

GREENLAND
Lowest population density in the world. Each person has 14.9 mi.^{2} (38.5 km^2).

NORTH AMERICA
POPULATION
351,659,000
5.09%
OF WORLD
POPULATION

67
Population of the country with the fewest people—the Pitcairn Islands in the middle of the Pacific Ocean.

LATIN AMERICA AND THE CARIBBEAN
POPULATION
588,649,000
8.52%
OF WORLD
POPULATION

AFRICA
POPULATION
1,033,043,000
14.95%
OF WORLD
POPULATION

ASIA
POPULATION
4,166,741,000
60.31%
OF WORLD POPULATION

MACAU, CHINA
Highest population density in the world. Each person has 0.00002 mi.^{2} (0.00005 km^2).

1,336,720,000

Population of the People's Republic of China, the country with the most citizens.

COUNTRIES THAT MAKE UP OCEANIA
POPULATION 35,838,000
0.52%
OF WORLD POPULATION

The ten countries with the largest number of people account for 58.7 percent of the world's population. The other countries—nearly 200—have just 41.3 percent.

58.7%   **41.3%**

CITY LIVING

Towns and cities are found in nearly every part of the world, from mountain peaks to arid deserts. Some are so large that more people live in them than in whole countries.

FIVE BIGGEST CITIES

The figures shown here represent the number of people found in each of these urban agglomerations. An agglomeration is a built-up area made up of the city and any suburbs that are linked to it.

2

DELHI
INDIA
22,157,000

Delhi is the largest agglomeration in terms of its area. Each person living here has an average space of 0.0006 mi.^{2} (0.0015 km^2).

5

MEXICO CITY
MEXICO
19,460,000

Nine million people live in Mexico City, with the rest living in neighboring areas.

3

SAO PAULO
BRAZIL
20,262,000

Covering an area of 3,089 mi.^{2} (8,000 km^2), Sao Paulo is the most populous city in the entire Americas.

4

MUMBAI
INDIA
20,041,000

Each person living in the agglomeration of Mumbai has an average of just 0.00002 mi.^{2} (0.00006 km^2).

NORTHERNMOST AND SOUTHERNMOST SETTLEMENTS

The Canadian settlement of Alert lies just 508 mi. (817 km) from the North Pole. At the other end of the Earth, Amundsen-Scott is an American scientific base at the South Pole.

Alert, Nunavut
Canada

Amundsen-Scott base
Antarctica

1
TOKYO
JAPAN
36,669,000

The Greater Tokyo Area is the largest agglomeration in the world. It is so big that it has swallowed other cities entirely, including Yokohama, which has 3 million people on its own.

In 1950, there were **83** cities with populations of more than **1 million** people. By **2007**, there were **468**.

LA RINCONADA, PERU
16,729 FT. (5,099 M)

HIGHEST AND LOWEST

The settlement of La Rinconada is close to a gold mine high up in the Andes Mountains. Despite the settlement's remote location, 30,000 people live and work there.

LA PAZ, BOLIVIA
11,942 FT. (3,640 M)

CUZCO, PERU
10,827 FT. (3,300 M)

DENVER, US
5,279 FT. (1,609 M)

SEA LEVEL

PARIS, FRANCE
115 FT. (35 M)

JERICHO, WEST BANK
ABOUT 820 FT. (250 M)
BELOW SEA LEVEL

9

REACH FOR THE SKY

Modern skyscrapers soar high into the air and are places where thousands of people live, work, shop, and even relax in parks and swimming pools.

BURJ KHALIFA ········>

The tallest building in the world contains:
160 hotel rooms,
27 acres (11 hectares) of park,
3,000 underground parking spaces,
and 26,000 panes of glass.

138 ft. (42 m)

The height of the world's first skyscraper, the Home Insurance Building, built in Chicago in 1885.

The Great Pyramid of Giza in Egypt was the tallest building in the world from 2570 BCE until 1311 CE. It is made from approximately 2.3 million stone blocks and weighs about 6.3 million tons.

GREAT PYRAMID GIZA, EGYPT
482 FT. (147 M)

TALLEST CITIES IN THE WORLD

These figures show the Calculated Average Height of the Ten Tallest (CAHTT) buildings in each city. In 2010, Dubai became the world's tallest city when the Burj Khalifa was officially opened.

DUBAI 1,150.6 FT. (350.7 M)

HONG KONG 1,081 FT. (329.5 M)

CHICAGO 1,036.4 FT. (315.9 M)

SHANGHAI 1,010.2 FT. (307.9 M)

GUANGZHOU 945.5 FT. (288.2 M)

NEW YORK CITY 940.9 FT. (286.8 M)

BURJ KHALIFA, DUBAI, UNITED ARAB EMIRATES
2,722.6 FT. (829.84 M)

CN TOWER, TORONTO, CANADA
1,815.4 FT. (553.33 M)

WILLIS TOWER, CHICAGO, UNITED STATES
1,729 FT. (527 M)

TAIPEI 101, TAIPEI, TAIWAN
1,670.6 FT. (509.2 M)

PETRONAS TOWERS, KUALA LUMPUR, MALAYSIA
1,482.6 FT. (451.9 M)

The two Petronas Towers in Kuala Lumpur, Malaysia, are linked by a bridge at the 41st and 42nd floors.

EIFFEL TOWER
PARIS, FRANCE
1,063 FT. (324 M)

2,500,000
The number of rivets used to build the Eiffel Tower.

RICH WORLD, POOR WORLD

Trade spreads money and wealth around the world. But this wealth is not spread evenly—some countries are very poor, while others can afford to borrow enormous amounts of money.

WHERE ARE THE RICH?

This map shows the percentage of the world's wealth held by different areas around the globe.

NORTH AMERICA 28%

SOUTH AMERICA 4%

THE RICHEST 0.5% OF THE WORLD'S POPULATION OWNS 38.5% OF ITS WEALTH. THE POOREST TWO-THIRDS OWNS JUST 3.3%.

WORLD TRADE

Countries need to buy certain goods from other parts of the world—this is called importing. The graphics below show the countries that import the highest value of goods.

90% The amount of the world's trade that is shipped around the globe by sea.

US 2,314,000,000,000

CHINA 1,743,000,000,000

Import levels 2011 (US$).

US$1.7 TRILLION

The amount the public debt of the United States increased by in 2010. It rose by US$1.9 trillion in 2009 and US$1 trillion in 2008.

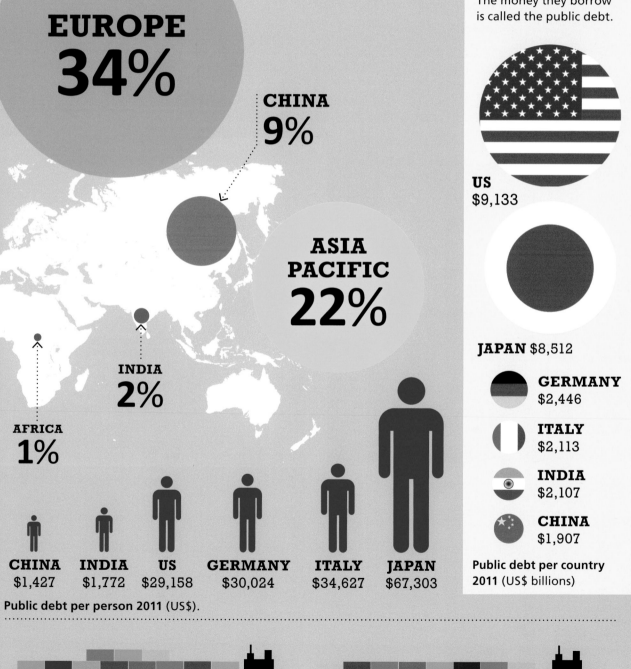

EUROPE 34%

CHINA 9%

ASIA PACIFIC 22%

INDIA 2%

AFRICA 1%

CHINA	INDIA	US	GERMANY	ITALY	JAPAN
$1,427	$1,772	$29,158	$30,024	$34,627	$67,303

Public debt per person 2011 (US$).

WHO OWES WHAT?

Countries may need to borrow money, for example, in order to build hospitals or buy weapons for their armed forces. The money they borrow is called the public debt.

US $9,133

JAPAN $8,512

GERMANY $2,446

ITALY $2,113

INDIA $2,107

CHINA $1,907

Public debt per country 2011 (US$ billions)

GERMANY 1,198,000,000,000

JAPAN 794,700,000,000

13

GOING **GLOBAL**

Some of the world's biggest corporations earn more money each year than entire countries. These companies employ thousands, sometimes millions, of people around the globe.

World's largest companies, third quarter 2011 (US$ millions)

APPLE 353,518.1
TECHNOLOGY HARDWARE, SOFTWARE, AND EQUIPMENT

EXXON MOBIL 353,135.2
OIL AND GAS PRODUCERS

PETROCHINA 276,473.9
OIL AND GAS PRODUCERS

IBM 208,843.5
SOFTWARE AND COMPUTER SERVICES

MICROSOFT 208,534.9
SOFTWARE AND COMPUTER SERVICES

BIG EARNERS

The figures in this graphic compare the market value of the world's largest companies. This value is based on the total value of their shares as they are bought and sold at stock exchanges around the world.

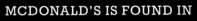

MCDONALD'S
This burger chain sells more than

75

hamburgers every single second and serves about

62,000,000

people every day—that's nearly twice the population of Canada.

MCDONALD'S IS FOUND IN

119

COUNTRIES.

GLOBAL EXPOSURE

The figures below show the percentage of the world in which the most globally widespread companies operate, employ people, or sell their goods and services.

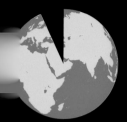

XSTRATA
Mining and quarrying 93.2%

ABB LTD
Engineering services 90.4%

NOKIA
Electrical and electronic equipment 90.3%

EXXON MOBIL
Oil and gas production 68%

T
Car

WALMART
LARGEST PRIVATE EMPLOYER IN THE WORLD. IT HAS

8,500

STORES IN 15 COUNTRIES UNDER 55 DIFFERENT NAMES. THESE NAMES INCLUDE WAL-MART, ASDA, SEIYU, AND BEST PRICE.

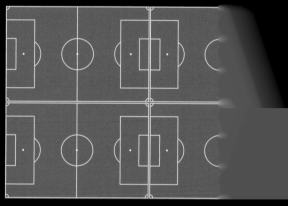

The largest Walmart store is in Albany, New York. It covers 260,000 ft.² (24,154.8 m²)—an area as large as 3.5 soccer fields.

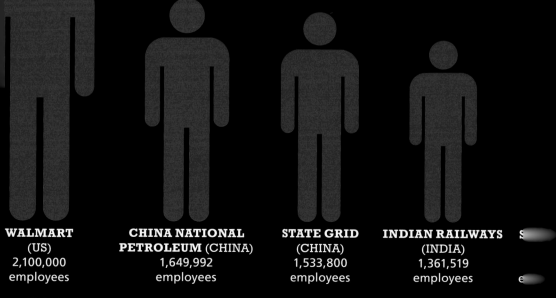

WALMART
(US)
2,100,000
employees

CHINA NATIONAL PETROLEUM (CHINA)
1,649,992
employees

STATE GRID
(CHINA)
1,533,800
employees

INDIAN RAILWAYS
(INDIA)
1,361,519
employees

S

e

WORLD'S BIGGEST EMPLOYERS 2011 (NOT INCLUDING NON-CORPORATE PUBLIC EMPLO

WATER

Without water, life would not be possible. But not everyone has access to safe water, while other people pour thousands of liters of water down the drain every year.

OF ALL THE WORLD'S WATER...

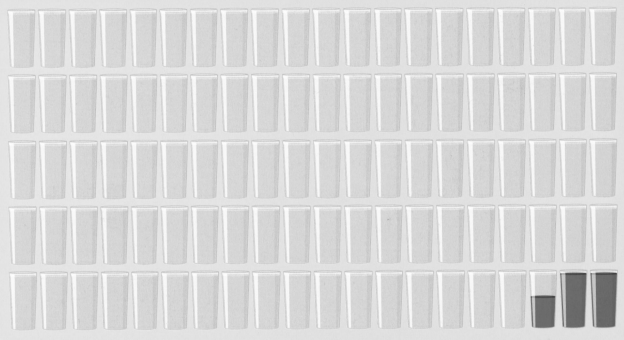

ACCESS TO WATER

Processing water to make it safe to drink is expensive, and many countries can't afford to supply their population with safe water. According to the World Health Organization, 884 million people don't have access to a safe water supply—that's nearly three times the population of the United States.

2.5%
IS FRESHWATER

OF THAT, ONLY
30%
is usable water. The remainder of the freshwater is locked in glaciers.

50 billion bottles of water are bought in the United States every year, creating **US$30 billion** in sales.

According to the United Nations, this amount of money would be enough to provide everyone on the planet with access to safe water.

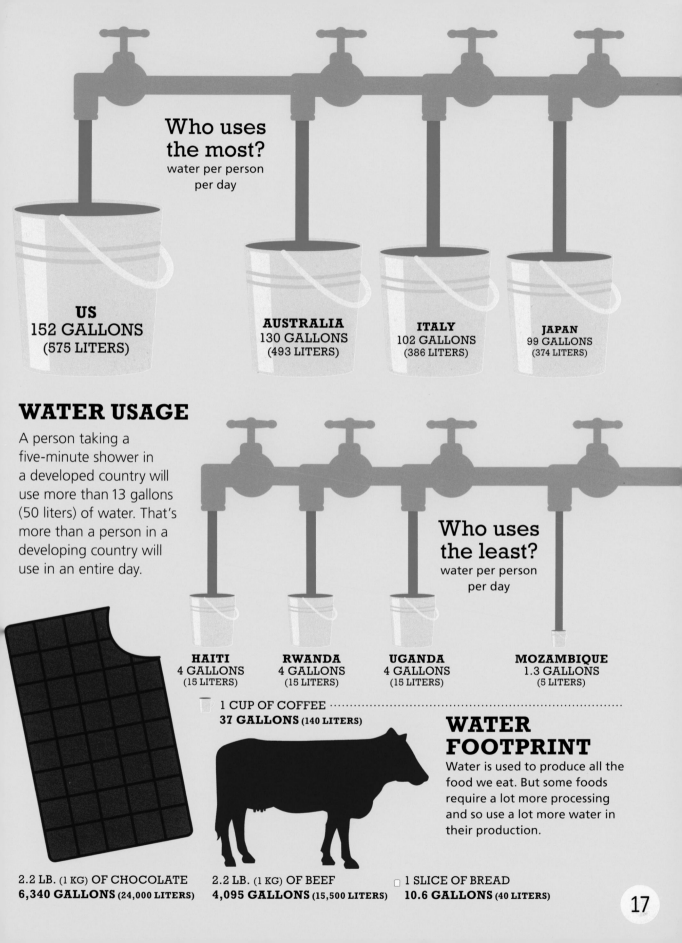

Who uses the most?
water per person per day

US
152 GALLONS
(575 LITERS)

AUSTRALIA
130 GALLONS
(493 LITERS)

ITALY
102 GALLONS
(386 LITERS)

JAPAN
99 GALLONS
(374 LITERS)

WATER USAGE

A person taking a five-minute shower in a developed country will use more than 13 gallons (50 liters) of water. That's more than a person in a developing country will use in an entire day.

Who uses the least?
water per person per day

HAITI
4 GALLONS
(15 LITERS)

RWANDA
4 GALLONS
(15 LITERS)

UGANDA
4 GALLONS
(15 LITERS)

MOZAMBIQUE
1.3 GALLONS
(5 LITERS)

1 CUP OF COFFEE
37 GALLONS (140 LITERS)

WATER FOOTPRINT

Water is used to produce all the food we eat. But some foods require a lot more processing and so use a lot more water in their production.

2.2 LB. (1 KG) OF CHOCOLATE
6,340 GALLONS (24,000 LITERS)

2.2 LB. (1 KG) OF BEEF
4,095 GALLONS (15,500 LITERS)

1 SLICE OF BREAD
10.6 GALLONS (40 LITERS)

WHAT A **WASTE!**

Humans are very wasteful and throw away millions of tons of useful food and materials every year. With more careful use, everyone on the planet could be fed with what's discarded.

WHERE DOES IT GO?

The vast amount of material thrown away each year could be recycled and used again. However, most of it is used only once and then discarded in landfill or burned in incinerators.

TRASH TREATMENT AROUND THE WORLD

54%
LANDFILL

24%
RECYCLED

12%
INCINERATED

8%
COMPOSTED

2%
OTHER

84% COULD BE RECYCLED

NEW YORK CITY PRODUCES 12,125 TONS OF TRASH A DAY.
In our lifetime, 307 million Americans will produce 9,888 billion cubic feet (280 billion cubic meters)

Only **20%** of the **29.8 billion** plastic bottles bought in the United States each year are recycled. Recycling the other **80%** could save **US$1.2 billion**, based on a price of 5 cents per bottle.

THE CITY OF GUIYU IN CHINA IS THE CENTER OF A HUGE ELECTRONICS RECYCLING INDUSTRY. EACH YEAR, **5,500** COMPANIES IN THE CITY EMPLOY ABOUT **150,000** PEOPLE TO DISMANTLE COMPUTERS, CELL PHONES, AND OTHER ELECTRONIC DEVICES. THIS ELECTRONIC WASTE, HOWEVER, RELEASES ELEMENTS INTO THE ENVIRONMENT THAT ARE HARMFUL TO PEOPLE AND NATURE.

70%

It takes 70 percent less energy to make recycled paper than to make paper from raw materials.

1974
900 CALORIES OF FOOD WASTED PER PERSON PER DAY

TODAY
1,400 CALORIES OF FOOD WASTED PER PERSON PER DAY

9,149,184

tons of food is wasted in the United Kingdom every year.

30.8% OF ALL FOOD PURCHASED IN THE UNITED KINGDOM IS THROWN AWAY.

2,000,000,000

people could be fed with the amount of food the United States throws away each year.

DWINDLING
RESOURCES

Humans take resources out of the ground and use them in nearly everything that's manufactured. However, unless we change the current rate of consumption, many of these resources will run out within fifty to seventy years.

GLOBAL OIL CONSUMPTION =
3.6 BILLION
BARRELS PER DAY

OIL: WHO USES THE MOST?
(barrels per day)

OIL RESERVES =
1.3 TRILLION BARRELS

US
19,150,000

CHINA
9,189,000

OIL WILL RUN OUT IN
2053

JAPAN
4,452,000

INDIA
3,182,000

RUSSIA
2,937,000

ISLAND OF NIUE 40

USING RESOURCES

Everything you use, whether it is a car, a cell phone, or a watch, needs resources to make it. We also use resources to power our homes, factories, and workplaces.

THE RICHEST 20% OF PEOPLE CONSUME 83% OF RESOURCES.

THE POOREST 20% OF PEOPLE CONSUME 1.3% OF RESOURCES.

435

The number of nuclear reactors around the world at the start of 2012.

PHOSPHORUS (FERTILIZER, ANIMAL FEED) 345 YEARS

TANTALUM (CELL PHONES, CAMERA LENSES) 116 YEARS

NICKEL (BATTERIES, TURBINE BLADES) 90 YEARS

URANIUM (WEAPONS, NUCLEAR POWER STATIONS) 59 YEARS

COPPER (WIRE, COINS, PLUMBING) 61 YEARS

GOLD (JEWELRY, DENTAL) 45 YEARS

LEAD (PIPES, BATTERIES) 42 YEARS

TIN (CANS, SOLDER) 40 YEARS

OTHER RESOURCES: WHEN WILL THEY GO?
Years remaining of mineral reserves, as of December 2011

COAL PROVIDES NEARLY **30%** OF THE WORLD'S ENERGY NEEDS, INCLUDING POWER AND HEATING...

...AND IS USED TO GENERATE MORE THAN **40%** OF THE WORLD'S ELECTRICITY.

GETTING AROUND

Today, nearly every person on the planet has access to some form of transport, whether it's a car for short journeys or a passenger jet to fly around the world. However, an increase in traveling has a huge impact on the environment.

CAR PRODUCTION

In 2010, 58,478,810 cars were built around the world. The biggest manufacturers were:

CHINA
13,897,083

JAPAN
8,307,382

GERMANY
5,552,409

SOUTH KOREA
3,866,206

BRAZIL
2,828,273

INDIA
2,814,584

US
2,731,105

CAR WORLD

The most popular car model is the Toyota Corolla from Japan. Since it was first sold in 1966, 32 million have been produced around the world.

THERE ARE APPROXIMATELY
600,000,000
PASSENGER CARS IN THE WORLD TODAY. THAT'S ONE FOR EVERY 11 PEOPLE.

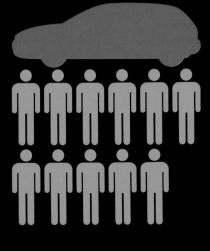

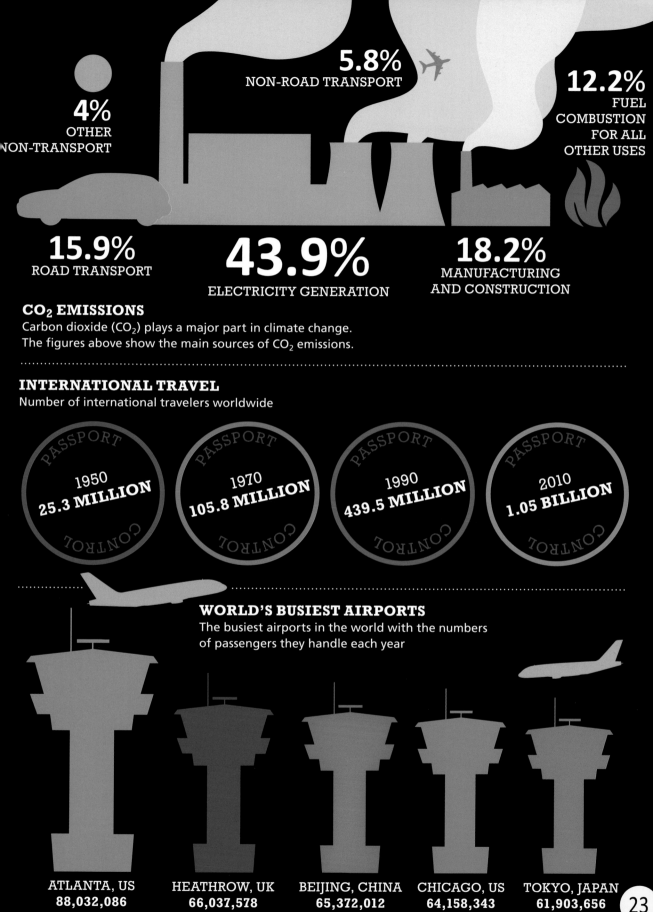

5.8%
NON-ROAD TRANSPORT

12.2%
FUEL COMBUSTION FOR ALL OTHER USES

4%
OTHER NON-TRANSPORT

15.9%
ROAD TRANSPORT

43.9%
ELECTRICITY GENERATION

18.2%
MANUFACTURING AND CONSTRUCTION

CO₂ EMISSIONS

Carbon dioxide (CO_2) plays a major part in climate change. The figures above show the main sources of CO_2 emissions.

INTERNATIONAL TRAVEL

Number of international travelers worldwide

PASSPORT CONTROL
1950
25.3 MILLION

PASSPORT CONTROL
1970
105.8 MILLION

PASSPORT CONTROL
1990
439.5 MILLION

PASSPORT CONTROL
2010
1.05 BILLION

WORLD'S BUSIEST AIRPORTS

The busiest airports in the world with the numbers of passengers they handle each year

ATLANTA, US
88,032,086

HEATHROW, UK
66,037,578

BEIJING, CHINA
65,372,012

CHICAGO, US
64,158,343

TOKYO, JAPAN
61,903,656

WORK, REST, AND PLAY

Travelers can affect the economy of the countries they visit through the money they bring with them. How much people travel depends on the number of hours they work and the amount of leave they can take.

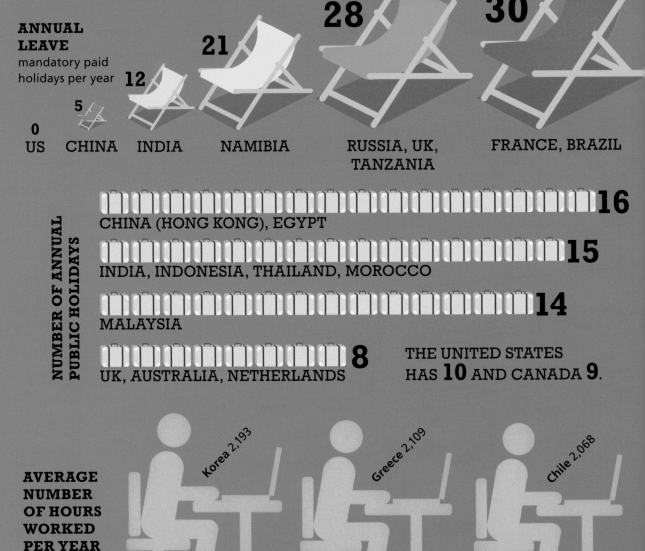

ANNUAL LEAVE
mandatory paid holidays per year

0	5	12	21	28	30
US	CHINA	INDIA	NAMIBIA	RUSSIA, UK, TANZANIA	FRANCE, BRAZIL

NUMBER OF ANNUAL PUBLIC HOLIDAYS

16 CHINA (HONG KONG), EGYPT

15 INDIA, INDONESIA, THAILAND, MOROCCO

14 MALAYSIA

8 UK, AUSTRALIA, NETHERLANDS

THE UNITED STATES HAS **10** AND CANADA **9**.

AVERAGE NUMBER OF HOURS WORKED PER YEAR

Korea 2,193

Greece 2,109

Chile 2,068

MOST POPULAR TOURIST COUNTRIES
International tourist arrivals

France 76.8 million
US 59.7 million
China 55.7 million
Spain 52.7 million
Italy 43.6 million
UK 28.1 million

IN 2010, INCOME FROM INTERNATIONAL TOURISM GREW TO **US$919 BILLION** WORLDWIDE—THAT'S MORE THAN THE ENTIRE COUNTRY OF TURKEY EARNS IN A YEAR.

TOURISM INCOME
Top three biggest earners from the tourist industry (US$ billions)

US 103.5
SPAIN 52.5
FRANCE 46.3

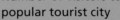

LOUVRE
7.5 MILLION

SACRÉ-COEUR
8 MILLION

EIFFEL TOWER
6.7 MILLION

CENTRE POMPIDOU
5.1 MILLION

DISNEYLAND PARIS
10.6 MILLION

VERSAILLES
3.45 MILLION

NOTRE DAME
12 MILLION

POPULAR DESTINATIONS IN PARIS
Number of visitors to attractions in the world's most popular tourist city

US 1,778
Japan 1,733
UK 1,647
France 1,554
Netherlands 1,377

25

STAYING IN TOUCH

The first writing appeared more than 5,000 years ago. Since then, many amazing inventions have greatly changed the way we communicate, allowing us to send messages around the globe in the blink of an eye.

THE INTERNET

The number of people using various languages on the internet

ENGLISH
536,000,000

CHINESE
509,000,000

SPANISH
164,000,000

LANGUAGES

There are thought to be up to 7,000 different languages spoken around the world. The figures below show the most popular first languages as a percentage of the world's population.

MANDARIN CHINESE 12.44%

SPANISH 4.85%

ENGLISH 4.83%

ARABIC 3.25%

HINDI 2.68%

THE REST 71.95%

832

The number of different languages spoken in Papua New Guinea.

TALKING LONG DISTANCE

Key moments in the history of long-distance communication:

HUMAN RUNNER
In 490 BCE, Pheidippides ran 140 mi. (225 km) from Athens to Sparta in two days, with news of the Battle of Marathon.

SEMAPHORE TOWERS
The arms on these towers move to form codes that spell out messages. They were used throughout western Europe by Napoleon in the early 19th century.

MORSE CODE
Using dots and dashes, the first morse code signal was sent on January 6, 1838.

PONY EXPRESS
This delivery service reduced message delivery time across the United States from several weeks to just 10 days.

AIRMAIL
The first official airmail delivery was on August 17, 1859. John Wise piloted a balloon from Lafayette, Indiana, to New York City.

TELEPHONE
The first call was made by Alexander Graham Bell on March 10, 1876.

WIRELESS
The first transatlantic radio message was sent in 1901.

MOBILE PHONE
The first call from a mobile phone was made on April 3, 1973.

In 2010, there were some **5.3 billion** cell phones in use. The countries with the greatest number of users were China with **747,000,000** and India with **670,000,000**.

GOING POSTAL
300,000,000,000
letters are posted each year around the world.

OTHER ITEMS 34%

LETTERS 66%

PROPORTION OF ITEMS POSTED EACH YEAR

5,500,000,000
letters are sent internationally.

4,000,000,000
of these are carried by plane.

THE DIGITAL
WORLD

The first e-mail was sent in 1971. Today, we type and send nearly 400 times as many e-mails as we do written letters.

RISE OF THE COMPUTER
The number of computers has more than doubled since the start of the 21st century.

2000 **140.2 MILLION**

2010 **350.9 MILLION**

E-MAIL
There are **3,150,000,000** known e-mail accounts in the world.

25% of these are company accounts.

THE WORLD'S FIRST PROGRAMMABLE, FULLY AUTOMATIC COMPUTING MACHINE WAS THE ZUSE Z3, BUILT IN 1941.

In 2011, there were **2,110,000,000** internet users around the world. China had **485,000,000**, while the United States had **245,000,000**.

By the end of 2011, there were **555,000,000** websites, of which some **300,000,000** had been created that year alone.

107,000,000,000,000
E-MAILS WERE SENT IN 2010...

89%
WERE SPAM.

You Tube™

35 HOURS
of video are uploaded to YouTube every minute.

KEEP TAKING THE TABLETS
How the type of computer we use will change worldwide

| 2008 FIGURES | | 2015 PROJECTIONS |

DESKTOP
45% → 18%

f

800,000,000
people were using Facebook by the end of 2011. More than 200 million of these signed up in that year.

LAPTOP
45% → 42%

36,000,000,000
photos are uploaded to Facebook every year.

NETBOOK/MINI PC
9% → 17%

TABLET
1% → 23%

250,000,000
tweets were sent every day during 2011.

GLOSSARY

Airmail
Letters, parcels, and other mail that is delivered by air, usually between different countries.

Agglomeration
A continuous built-up area, which may be made up of several towns and cities that are joined by suburbs and other urban areas.

Composted
When biodegradable materials, such as organic waste, are allowed to rot. This produces compost that can be used to feed crops and gardens.

Corporation
A very large company or group of companies.

Global exposure
The amount of the world where a company operates and employs people.

Debt
The amount of money that is owed by a person, company, or even an entire country.

Incinerated
When something is destroyed by burning it.

Landfill
A large hole in the ground into which waste and refuse are dumped and then covered over.

Mandatory
Something that has to happen. Mandatory holidays are days off that companies have to give their workers.

Market value
The total value of a company. This is decided by the value of the company's shares as they are bought and sold at stock markets in various parts of the world.

Morse code
An alphabet that uses a system of dots and dashes to represent letters. Morse code signals can be sent using a light or as pulses along electric wires.

ne people who live in a particular area, such as a country.

Population density
The number of people living in a particular area.

Public debt
The amount of money owed by a country's government.

Public holidays
Holidays that are taken to celebrate occasions that are important to a whole country or a specific group of people.

Resources
Materials that can be used to produce goods or energy. These can include natural resources, such as coal, oil, and minerals, and human resources, such as the size of a workforce.

Semaphore
A system of sending messages using large mechanical arms or flags. The positions of the arms and flags spell out different letters.

A small portion of a company that can be bought or sold by people or other companies. The total worth of a company's shares decides the company's market value.

Stock exchange
A place where company shares and other economic products are bought and sold.

Tablet
A small computer device that just has a screen and does not require a physical keyboard. Instructions can be typed directly onto the screen, which is touch-sensitive.

Trade
The buying and selling of goods between different peoples, regions, and countries.

Urban
Relating to towns, cities, and other built-up areas.

Resources

MORE GRAPHICS:
www.visualinformation.info
A website that contains a whole host of infographic material on subjects as diverse as natural history, science, sport, and computer games.

www.coolinfographics.com
A collection of infographics and data visualizations from other online resources, magazines, and newspapers

www.dailyinfographic.com
A comprehensive collection of infographics on an enormous range of topics that is updated every single day!

MORE INFO:
www.kids.nationalgeographic.com/kids/places/
Part of the children's section of the National Geographic website. This offers lots of information about different countries.

www.cyberschoolbus.un.org/
The educational web page for the United Nations. It includes an interactive database with the latest facts and statistics from around the world.

https://www.cia.gov/kids-page
The children's section of the website for the CIA. It provides links to information about the population and economy of every country on the planet.

The following sources were consulted to create this book:
Environmental Protection Agency; CIA World Factbook; United Nations; *Encyclopedia Britannica*; Credit Suisse Global Wealth report; *Financial Times*; *Fortune Magazine*'s Global 500; United Nations Conference on Trade and Development 2008; World Water Assessment Programme 2006; World Wildlife Fund; Pacific Institute; BP Statistical Review of World Energy 2010; World Bank; Organisation for Economic Co-operation and Development (OECD); United Nations World Tourism Organization; www.burjkhalifa.ae; www.waterfootprint.org

INDEX

Publisher of Chirp, chickaDEE and OWL
www.owlkidsbooks.com

Published in North America in 2013
© 2012 Wayland

All rights reserved. No part of this publication may be reproduced, stored in a retrieval system, or transmitted in any form or by any means, without the prior written permission of Owlkids Books Inc., or in the case of photocopying or other reprographic copying, a license from the Canadian Copyright Licensing Agency (Access Copyright). For an Access Copyright license, visit www.accesscopyright.ca or call toll-free to 1-800-893-5777.

Owlkids Books acknowledges the financial support of the Canada Council for the Arts, the Ontario Arts Council, the Government of Canada through the Canada Book Fund (CBF) and the Government of Ontario through the Ontario Media Development Corporation's Book Initiative for our publishing activities.

Published in Canada by
Owlkids Books Inc.
10 Lower Spadina Avenue
Toronto, ON M5V 2Z2

Published in the United States by
Owlkids Books Inc.
1700 Fourth Street
Berkeley, CA 94710

Library and Archives Canada Cataloguing in Publication

Richards, Jon, 1970-
    The human world / written by Jon Richards ; illustrated by
Ed Simkins.

(The world in infographics)
Includes bibliographical references and index.
ISBN 978-1-926973-94-4

    1. Human beings--Juvenile literature. I. Simkins, Ed II. Title.
III. Series: World in infographics

GN31.5.R53 2013   j301   C2012-908498-0

Library of Congress Control Number: 2013930496

Manufactured in Hong Kong, in February 2013, by Printing Express Ltd.
Job #13-01-018

A   B   C   D   E   F